THE LINDBERGH BABY KIDNAPPING TRIAL

A Primary Source Account

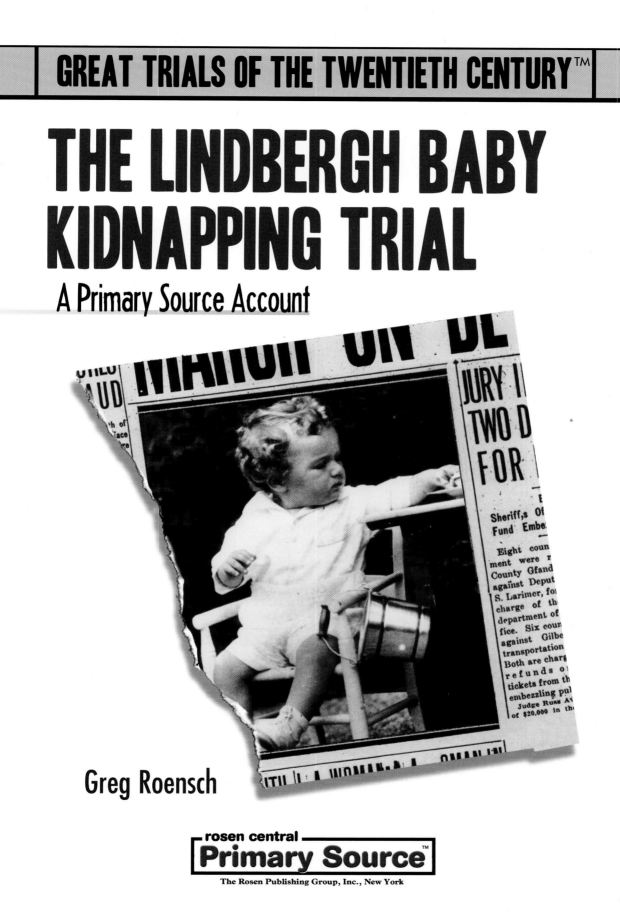

Greg Roensch

rosen central

Primary Source™

The Rosen Publishing Group, Inc., New York

Published in 2004 by The Rosen Publishing Group, Inc.
29 East 21st Street, New York, NY 10010

First Edition

Unless otherwise attributed, all quotes in this book are excerpted from court transcripts.

Library of Congress Cataloging-in-Publication Data

Roensch, Greg.
The Lindbergh baby kidnapping trial: a primary source account/by Greg Roensch.
    p. cm.—(Great trials of the twentieth century)
Includes bibliographical references and index.
ISBN 0-8239-3971-5 (libr. binding)
1. Trials (Kidnapping)—New Jersey. 2. Trials (Murder)—New Jersey.
[1. Hauptmann, Bruno Richard, 1899–1936—Trials, litigation, etc.
2. Lindbergh, Charles Augustus, 1930–1932—Kidnapping, 1932.]
I. Title. II. Series.
KF223.L53 R64 2003
345.73'0254—dc21
                       2002153352

Manufactured in the United States of America

CONTENTS

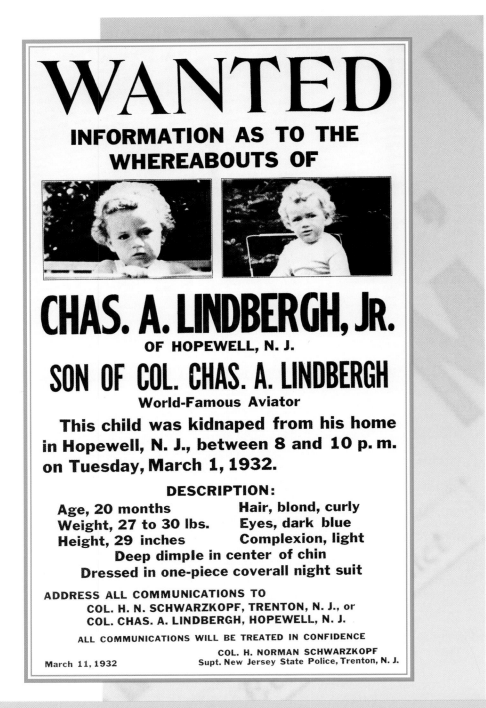

The kidnapping of Charles Lindbergh Jr. from his home on March 1, 1932, shocked the entire nation. The U.S. Justice Department became involved by printing up "wanted" posters and distributing them to police chiefs of more than 1,400 cities in the United States. The poster, created in March 1932, asked for any information regarding the case.

INTRODUCTION

Nothing seemed out of the ordinary at the Lindbergh house on the evening of March 1, 1932. By 10:00 PM, world-famous aviator and American hero Charles Lindbergh had finished dinner and was working in his library. His wife, Anne, was upstairs getting ready for bed. And in the nursery their young son, Charles Jr., was thought to be sleeping quietly. Within the next few minutes, their lives would change forever. At some point during the evening, Charles Jr. was kidnapped from the Lindbergh house, setting the stage for what would become known as the Trial of the Century.

From the first telephone calls to the local and state police, the Lindbergh baby kidnapping became a news story bigger than all other news stories. While there were other newsworthy events happening at the time, such as the Great Depression and Adolf Hitler's rise to power in Germany, nothing generated as much media attention as the Lindbergh kidnapping. Charles Lindbergh's popularity, combined with the shocking notion that someone would kidnap the son of one of America's greatest heroes, made this the top news story of the day.

Twenty-five-year-old Charles Lindbergh poses in front of his airplane, the *Spirit of St. Louis*, in New York City on May 20, 1927. Although he got his start as a barnstorming daredevil, walking on airplane wings and performing other aerial stunts, he soon turned his attention to the then-dangerous field of airmail delivery. It wasn't long before he entered a competition to make the first nonstop solo flight across the Atlantic Ocean.

It had been only five years since Charles Lindbergh became the first person to fly across the Atlantic Ocean on a nonstop solo flight. Lindbergh's daring journey from New York to Paris turned him into an instant celebrity, a hero for millions of people around the world. People turned out by the hundreds of thousands—sometimes by the millions—to catch a glimpse of this new American celebrity. In New

York City, for instance, he received a ticker-tape parade with more than four million people cramming the streets in his honor. With that fame, however, came something else. After the flight, people wanted to know everything about Lindbergh, and reporters went to extreme lengths to find news stories about him.

The fame generated by his record-setting flight did not fade. Whether it was news of his business ventures, his wedding to Anne Spencer Morrow in 1929, the flights they took together around the globe, or the birth of their first son, the press sought to report everything about Charles Lindbergh. As the news spread that someone had kidnapped young Charles Jr., it became clear that Charles Lindbergh would once again attract an unprecedented amount of the world's attention.

THE MOST FAMOUS AMERICAN

In 1919, a hotel owner named Raymond Orteig offered $25,000 to the first person to fly nonstop from New York to Paris. By 1926, many aviators were planning to attempt the flight. One of them was Charles Lindbergh. Lindbergh believed he could accomplish this feat if he had a plane designed specifically for such a long-distance flight. While searching for investors to help him build a custom plane, Lindbergh spent much of his time planning the historic flight and thinking about all the things he would need to accomplish it. After finding a group of St. Louis, Missouri, businessmen to fund his dream plane, Lindbergh found a company called the Ryan Aeronautical Company in San Diego, California, who could build it.

In a plane named the *Spirit of St. Louis*, Lindbergh departed from Roosevelt Field in New York on May 20, 1927. He was in the air for more than thirty-three hours. At times during the flight, he was so low over the Atlantic that he could feel the spray of ocean water on his face. As Lindbergh flew through the night, people around the world tuned in their radios for word about this daring young aviator and his quest

This aerial photograph of Charles Lindbergh flying over Paris, France, was taken on May 21, 1927, just before the completion of his historic transatlantic flight. In addition to winning the Raymond Orteig Prize of $25,000, Lindbergh was awarded the Distinguished Flying Cross and the Congressional Medal of Honor. He became a hero in the United States.

to achieve something never done before. His adventure received an unprecedented amount of attention.

After flying more than 3,600 miles, Lindbergh finally touched down at Le Bourget airfield in Paris. A cheering mob of thousands of people rushed to greet the *Spirit of St. Louis*. Lindbergh stepped out of his plane, and it soon seemed as if the entire world took notice of his amazing accomplishment.

THE SPIRIT OF ST. LOUIS

Along with space capsules, fighter planes, and many other aerial treasures, Lindbergh's *Spirit of St. Louis* is on display at the Smithsonian Air and Space Museum in Washington, DC. There's nothing like seeing the small, one-person airplane to fully appreciate Charles Lindbergh's amazing accomplishment. As you look at the plane, take a few minutes to imagine what it would have been like to fly alone, nonstop, for more than thirty hours across the Atlantic Ocean. With crude instrumentation and nothing much more than your instinct to guide your way, how would it have felt to fly into history like Charles Lindbergh did on May 20, 1927?

INSTANT FAME

From the moment Lindbergh landed in Paris, his life changed dramatically. He attended parties and massive parades in his honor and received many prestigious awards. Everyone wanted to meet the courageous aviator, from kings and presidents to celebrities and powerful businessmen. Telegrams and letters arrived from all over the world. In addition to countless congratulatory notes, Lindbergh received business propositions and even marriage proposals. Within a short time, Lindbergh realized that he had stepped into the unimaginable glare of the public spotlight. He was an instant celebrity.

Upon his return to the United States, Charles Lindbergh was honored with a ticker-tape parade. This photograph was taken on Broadway in New York City on June 13, 1927. A shy and reserved person who hailed from a small town in Minnesota, Lindbergh was an unlikely person to receive a hero's welcome. After tragedy—in part brought on by his immense fame—struck his young family, Lindbergh retreated from the public eye.

The Lindbergh Baby Kidnapping Trial

After visiting a few European cities, Lindbergh and the *Spirit of St. Louis* returned to the United States aboard the ship U.S.S. *Memphis*. As was the case in Europe, Lindbergh's popularity at home was overwhelming. In an effort to promote the new business of commercial aviation, Lindbergh took the *Spirit of St. Louis* on a three-month U.S. tour, on which he visited cities in nearly every state. Millions of people came to see Lindbergh during the tour. As his celebrity status grew, the press sought to report his every move.

Anne Morrow Lindbergh was born in New Jersey on June 22, 1906, to a wealthy businessman and a poet/women's education advocate. Privileged, shy, and literary, Anne once wrote in her journal that she planned on marrying a hero. She lived an accomplished life as an author, the first U.S. licensed woman glider pilot, and an inductee into the National Women's Hall of Fame. The photograph above was taken with her husband on August 27, 1929, in Cleveland, Ohio.

In 1929, Lindbergh married Anne Spencer Morrow, the daughter of a successful business-man and U.S. ambassador to Mexico. Although two years had passed since his historic trans-atlantic flight, Lindbergh was still as popular as ever. He and Anne were able to arrange a secret wedding ceremony despite the fact that the press followed their every move. There wouldn't be many quiet days for the Lindberghs after that. Charles and Anne went on aerial expedi-tions all over the world, becoming even bigger celebrities as they flew from one country to another, promoting aviation, charting new air routes, and living a life of adventure in the skies.

This 1931 photograph, taken the year before his kidnapping and murder, shows the infant Charles Lindbergh Jr. surrounded by *(from left to right)* his grandmother, great-grandmother, and mother, Anne Morrow Lindbergh.

On June 22, 1930, Anne gave birth to the Lindberghs' first child, a son named Charles Jr. Like any other story involving Charles Lindbergh, this one gained the attention of the press. Though Lindbergh urged reporters to respect his family's privacy, this story was too big for the press to ignore. In the papers, the baby was soon referred to by a variety of names, including Baby Lindy and the Eaglet. Not long after the birth of their son, Charles and Anne purchased more than four hundred acres of property near the town of Hopewell, New Jersey. Far from the unwanted attention of the press (or so they thought), this was the place where the Lindberghs would build their dream house.

"THEY HAVE STOLEN OUR BABY"

CHAPTER 2

While waiting for their new house in Hopewell to be finished, the Lindberghs lived at Anne's parents' house in Englewood, New Jersey. On Saturday, February 27, 1932, while Charles was working in New York, Anne brought Charles Jr.— now almost two years old—to the nearly completed new house for a weekend getaway. The Lindberghs had hired a couple named Olly and Elsie Whateley to take care of the house, and the Whateleys were now living on the property. The Lindberghs had also hired a nursemaid named Betty Gow to take care of little Charles. As was often the case on these weekend visits to Hopewell, Gow stayed behind at the Englewood house.

During this particular visit to Hopewell, young Charles had come down with a cold. So, instead of returning to her parents' house on Monday, as was typically the routine on these weekend excursions, Anne decided to stay longer at Hopewell. She didn't want to drive back to Englewood with the sick child. By Tuesday the baby seemed to be getting over his illness, but now it was Anne's turn to wrestle with a cold. She decided to remain at Hopewell until they were all feeling better. Anne telephoned Betty Gow and asked her to come to Hopewell to help take care of the baby.

On the evening of March 1, 1932, Anne and Betty put Charles Jr. to bed. Before leaving him for the night, Betty quickly sewed a flannel sleeping suit for the baby to make sure he stayed warm during the chilly night. She outfitted the boy in the new garment and left him to sleep. At about 8:30 PM, Charles arrived from New York. He and Anne had dinner together, while little Charles slept soundly upstairs. Everything seemed to be as it should be.

After dinner, while Anne prepared to go to bed, Charles went to his library. In the meantime, Betty Gow checked on the boy to make sure he was sleeping peacefully. When she

The Lindbergh's nursemaid, Betty Gow, takes young Charles Lindbergh Jr. for a carriage ride in this still from a home movie, taken April 4, 1932. Gow and other servants were suspects in the kidnapping for a short time. Her examination on the stand was so rigorous that the Scottish native fainted in the courtroom.

entered the room, Betty couldn't hear any sound coming from the baby's crib, so she walked closer and bent down to listen for his breathing. She soon realized that the baby wasn't there. Rushing to Anne's room, Betty learned that the baby wasn't with his mother either. She then ran downstairs to see if Charles had brought the boy into the library. It seemed impossible, but neither of the parents had the boy. Sensing the urgency of the situation, Charles took his rifle from the closet. As Betty Gow later testified in court, Charles looked around the baby's room, turned to his wife and said, "Anne, they have stolen our baby."

After word of the Lindbergh baby kidnapping got out, the press descended upon the estate of America's greatest celebrity. This photograph, taken shortly after the kidnapping in 1932, shows reporters swarming around the Lindbergh home in Hopewell, New Jersey. Ironically, the Lindberghs were in the process of relocating to Hopewell in order to be away from the relentless media.

THE SEARCH FOR THE BABY

Lindbergh noticed an envelope on the windowsill in the corner of the boy's room. Not wanting to tamper with any evidence, he didn't open the envelope. Without wasting any time, he had Olly Whateley telephone the sheriff's office in Hopewell. Lindbergh also called the New Jersey State Police.

During the course of that night and into the next day, investigators arrived at the scene. As the news spread, more and more people began to show up, and within a short time hundreds of people had converged on the Lindbergh property. In addition to local and state police, reporters and curious spectators flocked to the scene. Though the police eventually secured the area around the house, it was later argued that evidence was lost or damaged because so many people were trampling through the grounds.

Even though the scene was chaotic, the police began to find some clues. They found a shoe print in the mud outside the nursery window. They also found parts of a ladder and a carpenter's chisel near the house. After searching for fingerprints on the envelope found in the nursery, the authorities gave the envelope to Lindbergh. It contained a ransom note asking for $50,000 for the boy's

Investigators rushed to the scene to examine the Lindbergh grounds. In the photo above, taken in March 1932 in Hopewell, New Jersey, a detective tests out the ladder used in the kidnapping.

safe return. The kidnapper indicated that he would contact Lindbergh later about how and where to make the exchange. In order for Lindbergh to know that future notes were authentic, the kidnapper marked this note with a unique symbol that would serve as the kidnapper's signature on any subsequent notes.

17

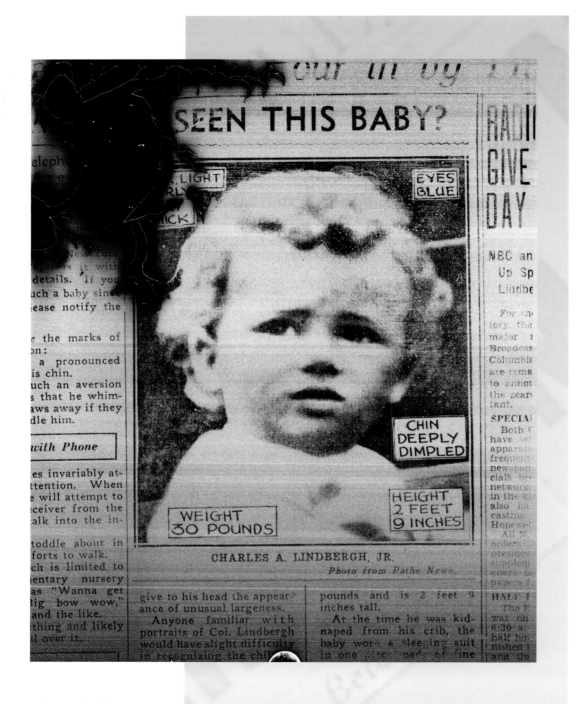

Pleas for any scrap of information available regarding the Lindbergh baby kidnapping were posted, printed, and broadcast all over the country. This clipping, from a March 1932 newspaper, shows a photograph of the young boy, with identifying references to his physical appearance.

LINDBERGH LEADS THE INVESTIGATION

From the night of the kidnapping and over the course of the next two and a half months, Lindbergh himself took control of the investigation. Setting up a headquarters in the garage of the Hopewell house, Lindbergh and the authorities followed any leads that came their way. There was tremendous public outrage that anyone could carry out such a crime against an admired American hero. The Lindberghs received offers of help and sympathy from a wide range of sources, from President Herbert Hoover to imprisoned gangster Al Capone.

Through all the confusion and commotion, Charles Lindbergh kept one thing in mind: He was determined to find his son no matter what it took. Following every lead and listening to anyone who had a story to tell about his son's possible whereabouts, Lindbergh focused all his attention on finding Charles Jr. One person who became involved early in the investigation and who would soon become a major figure in the case was Dr. John F. Condon.

Condon was a patriotic citizen who had become so angry about the kidnapping that he placed a letter in a New York newspaper saying that he'd be willing to do anything—even add some of his personal money to the ransom—to help get the Lindbergh baby back. Soon after placing the ad, Condon received a response from the kidnapper. In the letter, the kidnapper accepted Condon's offer to be the go-between and instructed him to contact Lindbergh. If Lindbergh agreed to the plan included in the note, he and Condon were instructed to place an ad in a New York newspaper saying, "Mony is redy." Condon arranged a meeting with Lindbergh, who agreed that Condon could act as a go-between.

JAFSIE AND CEMETERY JOHN

Condon and the kidnapper exchanged a series of notes, newspaper ads, and telephone calls. Since the kidnapper warned against involving the

Dr. John F. Condon (Jafsie), the man who offered to help Charles Lindbergh find the kidnapper of his baby, was photographed in Flemington, New Jersey, on December 27, 1934. Condon was a key witness for the prosecution, being the only one who could identify Cemetery John, the man who accepted the ransom money. Condon acted as a go-between and was the recipient of several ransom notes, a display of which is shown here with the kidnapper's special signature marking.

police, Condon used the code name Jafsie. On March 12, 1932, a taxi driver named Joseph Perrone delivered a note, which had been given to him anonymously, to Condon. It gave instructions for Condon to go to the main entrance of the Woodlawn Cemetery. At the cemetery, a man waved a white handkerchief to flag down Condon. Informing Condon that his name was John, he said that he was working as part of a gang of kidnappers who had taken the boy and were keeping him safe on a boat. As a token of proof that they really had the Lindbergh baby, John agreed to send the child's sleeping suit to Condon.

At the cemetery, John informed Condon that the kidnappers were increasing their ransom demand to $70,000 because of the growing publicity surrounding the case. Later, when told about the new demand, Lindbergh agreed to the higher payment. Condon, as he'd arranged with the kidnappers, then placed an ad in a newspaper to signal their acceptance of the plan. Within two days a package arrived containing the sleeping suit, which Lindbergh identified as the clothes the boy had been wearing on the night he disappeared. Condon urged Lindbergh to seek further proof that the baby was unharmed. Lindbergh didn't want to jeopardize the exchange, so he gave instructions to pay the ransom.

Before Condon and Lindbergh handed off the money, the police recorded the serial numbers on the bills so that they would be able to trace the money later if the kidnapper tried to spend it. They also used a currency called gold notes because gold notes were easier to spot than regular bills. Condon and Lindbergh later testified that on the night of April 2, 1932, they took $70,000 in two packages and went to meet the kidnapper. Parked by St. Raymond's Cemetery in New York City, they heard a voice calling "Ay, doctor" from across the street. Condon went to meet the man, whom he recognized as John. Lindbergh waited in the car. After talking John into accepting $50,000 instead of the agreed-upon $70,000, Condon paid the ransom. In return, he received an envelope containing instructions on where to find the boy. In the car, Lindbergh and Condon opened the envelope and read a note explaining that Charles Jr. could be found on a boat named the *Nelly* "between Horseneck Beach and Gay Head near Elizabeth Island."

Lindbergh flew up and down the Atlantic coast all night. Unfortunately, he couldn't find the *Nelly*. It began to dawn on him that they'd been fooled into paying the ransom and received nothing in return. After all the hard work and high hopes, their best lead had turned into nothing. Though he was discouraged, Lindbergh did not give up hope of finding his son. The investigation carried on. Then, roughly two and a half months after the boy's disappearance, two men driving near Hopewell made a gruesome discovery.

On May 12, 1932, the body of the Lindbergh baby was found not far from the Lindbergh house in Hopewell. After pulling off to the side of the road, two men noticed something strange in the woods. Upon closer inspection, they realized it was the decomposed remains of a young body. The police were summoned, and they determined that it was the body of Charles Lindbergh Jr. After months of investigations and communications with the supposed kidnappers, it turned out that the baby was not far from the house, dead from an apparent blow to the head.

THE SEARCH FOR THE KILLER

No longer looking for a kidnapper, the police now conducted a search for the boy's murderer. They looked at all possible suspects, including members of the Lindbergh and Morrow households. Betty Gow was among the people questioned and was eventually cleared of any wrongdoing. A maid named Violet Sharpe was also questioned. After behaving suspiciously during questioning, Sharpe was scheduled for

Examining evidence for the Lindbergh trial at the Hunterdon County Courthouse in Flemington, New Jersey, are assistant prosecutor Robert Peacock *(left)*, Hunterdon County prosecutor Anthony Hauck, an unidentified man, and New Jersey State Police captain John Lamb *(right)*, in this photograph taken January 3, 1935. Peacock holds the sleeping suit worn by the Lindbergh baby at the time of his kidnapping.

another interview. Before meeting again with authorities, however, Sharpe committed suicide. It seemed at first that this might be the break the police were waiting for, but it later turned out that she didn't have anything to do with the kidnapping. Neither Violet Sharpe nor Betty Gow nor anyone else employed by or otherwise associated with the Lindberghs was found to have any connection to the crime.

Soon after the ransom was paid, investigators began to notice that someone was spending the money. Unfortunately, it took nearly two years for the authorities to pick up solid leads on the marked money.

SCHWARTZKOPF

The chief of the New Jersey State Police, H. Norman Schwartzkopf, was the lead inspector for the Lindbergh kidnapping investigation. Because the initial ransom notes warned against involving the police, Charles Lindbergh insisted on leading the investigation himself. However, after the baby was found dead, Schwartzkopf led the investigation to hunt down the murderer. More than fifty years later, Schwartzkopf's son of the same name became famous as the commander in chief, central command, during the Persian Gulf War.

They knew the money was being spent in New York, but they didn't get a good lead until a bank employee noticed that one of the marked bills had a number written on it. The number, 4U-13-14 N.Y., turned out to be a license plate number that was written on the bill by a gas station attendant who had suspected that the note might be counterfeit. With the license number, the police were finally able to zero in on a suspect.

On September 19, 1934, after tracing the license plate number to a car owned by a German immigrant named Bruno Richard Hauptmann, police waited near Hauptmann's apartment. As he drove away in his car, the police followed him and soon pulled him over. In a short time, a group of policemen—with guns drawn—surrounded Hauptmann's car. While searching his wallet, the police found another of the marked gold notes. When asked about the notes, Hauptmann said that he had another three hundred of them at his house.

The man credited with tipping off authorities, Walter Lyle (*right*), is shown with fellow gas station attendant John Lyons, in this photograph, taken August 20, 1934, in New York City. Lyle took down Hauptmann's license plate number when Hauptmann paid for his gasoline with a gold certificate, an unusual form of payment.

GATHERING EVIDENCE

During the next few days, the police subjected Hauptmann to a grueling interrogation. They wanted to know more about the money and a chisel (like the one found at the crime scene) that was apparently the only tool

Bruno Richard Hauptmann is shown being fingerprinted after his arrest at New York City Police Headquarters, in this photograph from September 19, 1934. He was indicted nearly a month later. Upon his arrest and throughout his trial, Hauptmann maintained his innocence. Many people still believe he had no part in the kidnapping and death of Charles Lindbergh Jr.

missing from his tool chest, and they wanted information about a sketch of a ladder found in a notebook at Hauptmann's apartment.

At one point when Hauptmann was on the verge of collapse, the police asked him to provide handwriting samples so they could compare his writing to that in the ransom notes. Though the police harshly interrogated him, Hauptmann continued to maintain his innocence.

Even after police discovered more than $14,000 in marked money in his garage and caught him in a lie about how much of the money he had, Hauptmann continued to claim he didn't know anything about or have anything to do with the kidnapping.

The evidence continued to mount. Police brought in handwriting experts who claimed that Hauptmann's handwriting and the writing on the ransom notes were by the same person. They also brought in witnesses who worked against Hauptmann, such as Joseph Perrone, the cab driver who brought a note to John Condon. Perrone identified Hauptmann as the man who gave him the note to deliver. Another witness who identified Hauptmann was Charles Lindbergh. When hearing Hauptmann's voice, Lindbergh identified it as the voice he and Condon heard on the night they met John to exchange the ransom money at St. Raymond's Cemetery.

With evidence piling up against him and with so much interest by the police, the press, and the public to find someone responsible for this crime, the authorities finally indicted Hauptmann for first-degree murder. At Hauptmann's arraignment on October 23, 1934, Judge Thomas W. Trenchard read the charges and set a trial date for January 2 of the following year.

THE CASE FOR THE PROSECUTION

On January 2, 1935, the trial of *The State of New Jersey v. Bruno Richard Hauptmann* began in the Hunterdon County Courthouse in the town of Flemington, New Jersey. Flemington, or any town for that matter, had never seen anything like the gathering of reporters, spectators, and even celebrities who came to witness the Lindbergh kidnapping trial. With thousands of people arriving for the case, it seemed all at once as if this small town had become the center of the universe.

From the start of the proceedings, a crowd of spectators and reporters jammed into every inch of the courtroom. In less than two days, eight men and four women were chosen for the jury. Judge Thomas W. Trenchard instructed them against reading newspaper articles, listening to radio broadcasts, or attending public gatherings. He wanted them to understand that they should base their decision on the evidence presented in court and not on opinions they heard in the news or elsewhere. After the judge completed his remarks, it was time for the prosecution to deliver its opening statement.

New Jersey attorney general David T. Wilentz led the prosecution team. He stated the prosecution's objective: "[T]he State will prove to you that . . . a happy, normal, jovial, delightful little tot" was killed by Hauptmann. "He [Hauptmann] broke into and entered at night the Lindbergh home with the intent to steal that child and its clothing. And he did." According to New Jersey state law at the time, someone convicted of kidnapping could not receive the death penalty. However, someone found responsible for a death while committing burglary could be found guilty of first-degree murder and given the death penalty. Therefore, Wilentz argued that Hauptmann, if convicted of stealing the baby and the baby's clothes, should be sentenced to death.

During his forty-five-minute opening statement, Wilentz walked the jury through the events of the night of the kidnapping as he imagined them. He described how Hauptmann used a ladder to climb up to the second-floor nursery at the Lindbergh home. Then, according to Wilentz, the ladder broke while Hauptmann was descending with the baby in his arms. "And down he went with this child . . . It received a horrible fracture, the dimensions of which when you hear about it will convince you that death was instantaneous." Wilentz then explained how Hauptmann carried the already dead boy to the spot in the woods where he buried the infant in a shallow grave.

This photograph, taken on January 21, 1935, in Flemington, New Jersey, shows Judge Thomas W. Trenchard sitting in the Hunterdon County Courthouse. Trenchard was known for sticking to his rulings. When a prison inmate confessed to kidnapping the Lindbergh baby, Trenchard refused Hauptmann a stay of execution, noting the importance of allowing state courts to make decisions.

This diagram was sketched on March 2, 1932. The drawing notes the location of Charles and Anne Lindbergh, who were in the east wing of the house when their baby was kidnapped. It also depicts the other end of the mansion, where a ladder was placed against the west wall under a nursery window. At the time of this illustration, it was believed that a man and a woman had taken part in the kidnapping.

BETWEEN 7.30 AND 10 O'CLOCK KIDNAPER CARRIES SLEEPING BABY DOWN LADDER WHILE WOMAN ACCOMPLICE WAITS

WEST ⟶

TO LAMBERTVILLE AND THE DELAWARE RIVER.

It was clear, according to Wilentz, that Hauptmann committed the crime "because he wanted money—money—money—lots of money." Wilentz concluded his opening statement by telling the jury: "We will be asking you to impose the death penalty, it is the only suitable punishment in this case."

When Wilentz finished his statement, the lead attorney for the defense, Edward J. Reilly, objected to the prosecutor's opening remarks and asked the judge to declare a mistrial on the grounds that the prosecutor intended to unjustly prejudice the jury against his client. Though the judge did not declare a mistrial, he did remind the jurors to listen carefully to all of the evidence before making up their minds about the case.

WITNESSES FOR THE PROSECUTION

Over the course of the trial, the prosecution called eighty-seven witnesses, including experts and investigators, people who worked for the Lindberghs, and people who claimed to see Hauptmann near the scene of the crime. One of the first witnesses was Anne Lindbergh, who

Taken on January 3, 1935 in Flemington, New Jersey, this photograph shows Charles Lindbergh telling the court about the ransom notes he received. Lindbergh testified after his wife recounted her version of the events that took place the night of her baby's kidnapping. In contrast to his wife's emotional testimony, Lindbergh remained steady and convincing on the stand.

identified her son's clothes as well as a photograph of him and talked about the night of the disappearance. The defense declined to cross-examine her, saying, "The defense feels that the grief of Mrs. Lindbergh requires no cross-examination." Soon afterward, the prosecution called one of its most compelling witnesses—Charles Lindbergh.

During his testimony, Lindbergh answered questions about the moments, days, and weeks following the kidnapping; about how he had found the ransom note in the nursery; and about how he had done everything within his power to bring his son safely home. During the second day of Lindbergh's testimony, Wilentz asked him of the meeting at St. Raymond's Cemetery, "You heard a voice hollering, 'Aye, doctor,' I think. Since that time have you heard the same voice?" Lindbergh's response was powerful testimony against Hauptmann: "Yes, I have . . . That was Hauptmann's voice."

When defense attorney Reilly questioned Lindbergh during cross-examination, he tried to deflect blame from Hauptmann by asking Lindbergh about a range of other possible suspects, including Lindbergh's neighbors and servants. In the end, though, Reilly couldn't do anything to lessen the power of Lindbergh's testimony.

The prosecution called a number of other key witnesses whose testimony hurt Hauptmann's case. When Betty Gow was shown the boy's sleeping suit, she said, "This is the

Amandus Hochmuth points out Bruno Richard Hauptmann as the man he saw driving near the Lindbergh home with a ladder in his truck. Hochmuth testified that when Hauptmann realized that he had been seen, "he glared at me as if he saw a ghost." This photograph was taken during the Hauptmann trial in Flemington, New Jersey.

exact little shirt I made for the baby that night." Another witness, a man named Amandus Hochmuth who lived on the road leading to the Lindbergh house, claimed to have seen Hauptmann driving a car with a ladder in it on the day of the kidnapping. Yet another witness, the cab driver Joseph Perrone, identified Hauptmann as the man who had given him a note to deliver to John Condon. And Condon, when asked to identify the John he met in the cemetery, said, "John is Bruno Richard Hauptmann."

Handwriting analyst James Clark Sellers was one of many expert witnesses called to the stand by the prosecution during the Hauptmann trial in Flemington, New Jersey. Sellers pointed out strong similarities between the writing samples Hauptmann volunteered and the script on the ransom notes. "He might as well have signed the notes with his own name," Sellers said.

KEY EVIDENCE AGAINST HAUPTMANN

For nearly one month, the prosecution brought forth witnesses to prove its case against Hauptmann. Key prosecution evidence included analysis of Hauptmann's handwriting compared with the writing on the ransom notes. Eight handwriting experts testified for the prosecution that Hauptmann's writing was the same as the writing on the ransom notes. As part of their proof, the experts demonstrated how Hauptmann misspelled words that were also misspelled by the author of the notes. For

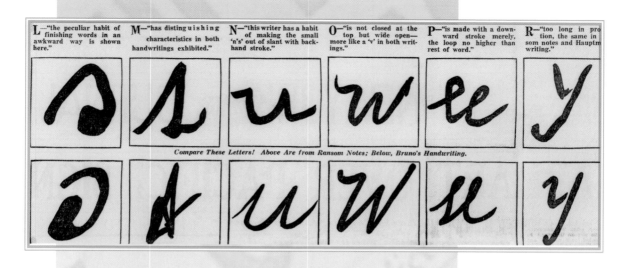

L—"the peculiar habit of finishing words in an awkward way is shown here."

M—"has distinguishing characteristics in both handwritings exhibited."

N—"this writer has a habit of making the small 'n's' out of slant with backhand stroke."

O—"is not closed at the top but wide open—more like a 'v' in both writings."

P—"is made with a downward stroke merely, the loop no higher than rest of word."

R—"too long in proportion, the same in som notes and Hauptm writing."

Compare These Letters! Above Are from Ransom Notes; Below, Bruno's Handwriting.

This detail of the expert witnesses' handwriting analysis charts shows the close matching of letters from the ransom notes (*top row*) and from Hauptmann's handwriting (*bottom row*). The image was taken on January 12, 1935, in Flemington, New Jersey. The handwriting experts were able to discover similarities such as uncrossed *t*'s and transposed letters making the word "the" into "hte."

example, "house" was spelled "haus," "note" was "not," "good" was "gut," "boat" was "boad," and so on.

Another key piece of evidence against Hauptmann was the ladder found at the crime scene. To prove Hauptmann's connection to the ladder, the prosecution called wood expert Arthur Koehler to the stand. Koehler had spent more than a year studying the ladder found at the Lindbergh house. Even before Hauptmann's arrest, Koehler had analyzed wood from lumberyards around the country in an attempt to track down the wood used to make the ladder. After his extensive research, Koehler calculated that the wood used to build the ladder had been purchased at the same lumberyard where Hauptmann, a carpenter, bought his wood. Furthermore, Koehler testified that part of the ladder was made from a piece of wood that was missing from the attic in Hauptmann's apartment.

In addition to the handwriting samples and the ladder, another key piece of evidence against Hauptmann was the ransom money.

New Jersey state trooper Joseph Bornmann carries the ladder found outside the Lindbergh home into the courtroom of Bruno Richard Hauptmann's trial. The ladder was a key piece of evidence in convicting Hauptmann. One of the ladder's rails matched the floorboards in Hauptmann's attic. In addition, the unusual square nails holding the rail to the ladder were also found in Hauptmann's attic.

Hauptmann had been linked to money spent at a movie theater and to the money spent at the gas station, which eventually led to his arrest. In addition to showing that Hauptmann had been spending the marked ransom notes, the prosecution also described how Hauptmann continued to lie about the money. As he got caught in one lie after another, it was clear that Hauptmann knew more about the money than he was saying. No matter how the defense tried to explain how Hauptmann had come into possession of this money, it was powerful evidence against him.

HAUPTMANN'S DEFENSE

After Arthur Koehler, the wood expert, completed his testimony, the prosecution rested its case. It was now the defense's turn to prove that Hauptmann was not the right man.

Lloyd Fisher, one of Hauptmann's four lawyers, delivered the opening statement. He presented an overview of the defense's strategy, saying that the defense would provide Hauptmann with an alibi for the night of the kidnapping as well as for other key dates. Also, he told the courtroom that the defense would bring its own handwriting experts who would show "there can't be a doubt in any of your minds that that is not the handwriting of Bruno Richard Hauptmann" on the ransom notes.

In his opening statement, Fisher also challenged the testimony of key prosecution witnesses, such as Amandus Hochmuth, and claimed that the police had poorly handled evidence such as the ladder. "We believe we will be able to show that no case in all of history was as badly mangled as this case." When he finished his opening remarks, Fisher turned the proceedings over to lead defense attorney, Edward J. Reilly. The defense called its first witness: Bruno Richard Hauptmann.

Bruno Richard Hauptmann stands with his defense attorneys at the Hunterdon County Courthouse in Flemington, New Jersey, in this photograph taken on January 3, 1935. *From left to right*: Edward Reilly, Lloyd Fisher, Frederick Pope, Hauptmann, and Edgar Rosencrans. Reilly was brought on board Hauptmann's defense team when a New York City newspaper offered to pay his salary in return for exclusive trial stories.

HAUPTMANN TAKES THE STAND

After listening for weeks to the evidence against him, Hauptmann now had the chance to tell his side of the story. Other than a few outbursts, like saying that Amandus Hochmuth was *verrückt* ("crazy" in German) and calling cab driver Joseph Perrone a liar, Hauptmann had for the most part sat quietly through the testimony against him. Now was his chance to set the record straight and explain in his own words why he wasn't responsible for the death of Charles Lindbergh Jr.

Over the next few days, Hauptmann would testify for about seventeen hours. He answered questions about his background in Germany, where he had served in the German army during World War I. After the war, Hauptmann had been unable to find a job in his war-torn country and had resorted to robbery to survive. He discussed this period and the jail time he'd served after being arrested for robbery. Hauptmann also discussed coming to America. After two failed attempts to reach the United States by stowing away aboard a ship, he described how he finally reached America on the third try. Since coming to America illegally, Hauptmann worked in a variety of jobs, most recently as a carpenter, and pursued other business ventures. In America, he had led a quiet, law-abiding life with his wife, Anna, and their young son, Manfred.

During the course of his testimony, Hauptmann sought to provide alibis for critical dates associated with the kidnapping case. On the day of the kidnapping, for instance, Hauptmann said that he had reported for his first day of work at a new job at an apartment building called the Majestic. Upon arrival at the job site, he found out that the job wouldn't start until a couple of weeks later. Unfortunately for Hauptmann, the employment records from the Majestic couldn't be located. Hauptmann didn't have a strong alibi for his whereabouts for the remainder of the day.

Another key date was April 2, the day when Charles Lindbergh and John Condon handed off the ransom money at St. Raymond's Cemetery. Again, Hauptmann claimed that he was working at the Majestic. This time, it was his last day on that job, which he was quitting because of a salary dispute. On the evening of April 2, Hauptmann went home and stayed there with his wife and a friend named Hans Kloppenburg. Kloppenburg "was playing the guitar and I was playing the mandolin, and we used to play together and enjoy ourselves for about an hour, hour and a half, to keep in practice." When questioned

In this posed photograph, taken in the library of the Hunterdon County Courthouse in Flemington, New Jersey, Edward Reilly acts out his examination on the stand of Bruno Richard Hauptmann. When asked if he had ever been to Hopewell, New Jersey, where the Lindberghs lived, Hauptmann replied, "I never was."

later, Anna Hauptmann confirmed this testimony, as did Kloppenburg. However, upon further questioning, Kloppenburg also admitted that he had previously been unsure of the exact date.

The third alibi date was November 26, 1933. It was on this night, according to testimony from an employee at a movie theater, that Hauptmann spent a marked ransom note to buy a ticket. Hauptmann denied this allegation, saying that it was his birthday on that day and he was celebrating at home with his wife and friends. Anna Hauptmann and some friends later testified that Hauptmann was with them at a small party on that night.

HAUPTMANN CONFRONTS KEY EVIDENCE

Throughout his entire testimony, Hauptmann maintained that he didn't have anything to do with the kidnapping and had never been anywhere near the Lindbergh house. When asked "Were you ever in Hopewell in your life?" Hauptmann replied, "I never was." Of course, Hauptmann would have to do more to prove his innocence than simply claim he'd never been at the Lindbergh estate. He would need to answer questions about the evidence against him.

He tried to explain his possession of the ransom money by saying that it belonged to a business associate named Isidor Fisch. Before leaving on a trip to Germany, Fisch had given a shoe box to Hauptmann. At the time Hauptmann did not know the contents of the shoe box. It was only later, while looking for a broom in his garage, that Hauptmann looked closely at the contents of the box and saw that it contained a large amount of money. Hauptmann claimed he eventually took some of the cash because Fisch had owed him money. Fisch could not back up Hauptmann's testimony because he had died while in Germany.

Another key piece of evidence against Hauptmann was the ladder. The defense led Hauptmann into a discussion about the quality of the ladder.

This photograph of Hauptmann's friend Isidor Fisch was taken sometime around 1935. Fisch was the mysterious dead man Hauptmann claimed had given him the shoe box of ransom money.

When asked if he built the ladder, Hauptmann responded, "[C]ertainly not . . . [it] looks like a music instrument . . . I don't know how a man can step up." Furthermore, Hauptmann testified that he never carried the ladder in his car.

Reilly also questioned Hauptmann about his handwriting samples. Hauptmann testified that the police had beaten him and forced him to spell words incorrectly so his writing matched the writing on the ransom notes. "They forced me. They said, 'You won't get any sleep, you got to write.'" Hauptmann made a mistake during this part of his testimony by claiming that the police forced him to misspell the word "signature." It turned out, however, that the police hadn't asked him to write that word at all. Moreover, when he spelled the word aloud in court, Hauptmann misspelled it in the same way it was misspelled on the ransom note.

When Reilly finished asking questions, it was the prosecution's turn to cross-examine the witness.

HAUPTMANN ON THE HOT SEAT

From the start of the prosecution's cross-examination, prosecuting attorney Wilentz went on the attack against Hauptmann, zeroing in on the fact that Hauptmann had been caught in a number of lies. "You have had an opportunity in this court today to tell the whole truth.

Have you told the truth?" Wilentz wanted the jury to think that if Hauptmann was lying about so many other things, then he was lying about his innocence in the case as well.

Wilentz questioned Hauptmann more about his background, focusing on his criminal past in Germany. Hauptmann was also made to answer more questions about his illegal entry into the United States. "Mr. Defendant, you came into this country illegally, didn't you?" All of the questions about his shady background painted a picture of Hauptmann as anything but the law-abiding citizen he appeared to be.

Another piece of evidence, a wooden plank taken from Hauptmann's garage, is shown above. Four holes drilled into the plank contained $860 of the ransom money and a loaded gun. Additional cash was found in a shellac can in the garage.

During the cross-examination, Wilentz also questioned Hauptmann further about his handwriting and his dealings with Isidor Fisch. Then Wilentz asked about a board that came from a closet in Hauptmann's home. On the board was written the phone number and address of Dr. John Condon. Earlier, Hauptmann had admitted that the writing was his. Now, however, he denied writing the address and phone number. Hauptmann admitted that he had made a mistake earlier when he said the writing was his. Again, this testimony put Hauptmann in a bad light, and it looked like he was caught in yet another lie.

At times throughout this cross-examination, Hauptmann and Wilentz had some heated exchanges. Wilentz was constantly on the attack, and Hauptmann was fighting for his life. At one point, Wilentz asked Hauptmann, "You think you are a big shot, don't you? . . . You think you are bigger than everybody, don't you?" Hauptmann shot back, "No, but I know I am innocent." Though Wilentz pushed hard to get Hauptmann to confess, the defendant never admitted to the crime. Hauptmann may have been caught in a number of lies, but he held his ground firmly in his assertion that he did not have anything to do with the Lindbergh kidnapping.

THE VERDICT

After Hauptmann's testimony, the defense called a number of witnesses in support of Hauptmann's alibis or to provide other testimony on his behalf. When questioned by Reilly, Anna Hauptmann confirmed her husband's alibis for key dates. However, upon cross-examination by Wilentz her answers weren't so convincing. Other witnesses were even less impressive, and Hauptmann at one point asked his attorney Lloyd Fisher, "Where are they getting these witnesses from? They're really hurting me."

About six weeks after the trial had begun, the attorneys for both sides delivered their closing arguments. For the defense, Edward J. Reilly summed up his client's position, saying that the evidence against Hauptmann was circumstantial. In other words, there was still nothing that absolutely proved Hauptmann was guilty of the crime. Reilly made an appeal to the jury to use their common sense to find Hauptmann innocent: "[T]his is the crime of the century. There isn't any doubt about it. Let's face this, because this case has come down to common ordinary horse sense." According to Reilly, the defense had provided alibis for crucial dates relating to the crime.

Reilly proceeded to speculate about other possibilities. He wondered aloud about the people who worked for the Lindberghs—perhaps one or more of them had something to do with the crime. Maybe it was Betty Gow. Or perhaps Violet Sharpe. He also suggested other possible conspirators, including John Condon and Isidor Fisch. Reilly argued that you could also find logical reasons to suspect any of these other people instead of his client.

The prosecution, on the other hand, had no doubt about Hauptmann's guilt. Wilentz reiterated his belief in Hauptmann's guilt, saying, "I have lost more weight in this case than the defendant, only because I wanted to be sure, to be certain, to be positive." Wilentz attacked Hauptmann. "Now what type of man would kill the child of Colonel Lindbergh and Anne Morrow? . . . He wouldn't be an American. No American gangster and no American racketeer ever sank to the level of killing babies. Ah, no! Oh, no, it had to be a fellow that had ice water in his veins, not blood." Wilentz attacked Hauptmann and responded in detail to Reilly's conclusions for the defense. In the end, Wilentz appealed to the members of the jury to do their duty: "Jurors, it is up to you. You have got a chance to do something for society that nobody else in the entire county of Hunterdon will ever have . . . it seems to me you have the courage, if you believe with us, you have to find him guilty of murder in the first degree."

When the attorneys on both sides finished delivering their closing statements, the judge gave final instructions to the jury. Finally, it was time for the twelve men and women of the jury to decide Hauptmann's guilt or innocence.

REACHING A VERDICT

The jury deliberated over the verdict for more than eleven hours. During that time, a crowd gathered outside the Hunterdon County Courthouse. Voicing the sentiment that had been felt against Hauptmann since his capture, the mob began to shout, "Kill

Taken on February 13, 1935, in the Flemington, New Jersey, courtroom where the Hauptmann trial was held, this photograph shows the jury delivering the verdict. Judge Trenchard had instructed the jury that even an accidental death, if occurring during a burglary, was a crime warranting the death penalty.

The Lindbergh Baby Kidnapping Trial

Hauptmann! Kill Hauptmann!" As time passed, the crowd continued to grow, reaching nearly seven thousand people. From his jail cell, Hauptmann could certainly hear that the mob had already reached its decision.

Behind the scenes, the jury had reached a verdict on its first vote. All twelve members of the jury found Hauptmann guilty. However, they did not initially agree that Hauptmann should receive the death penalty. So, while the jury continued to debate over Hauptmann's fate, the crowd outside continued to yell its opinion: "Kill Hauptmann! Kill Hauptmann!" Eventually, the jury returned to the courtroom and declared Hauptmann guilty of first-degree murder. Judge Trenchard then informed the courtroom that Hauptmann would suffer the ultimate penalty and be put to death for his crime. When the crowd outside the courtroom heard the news, they cheered.

The Lindberghs weren't in the courthouse when the verdict was announced. Instead, they had gone to Anne's parents' home, where they listened to radio reports from the scene. When the news of Hauptmann's guilt eventually came, Anne asked Charles to turn off the radio. Finally, their ordeal was over.

In the months after the trial, the Lindberghs tried to resume normal lives. By the end of the year, Anne had published her first book, *North to the Orient*, which became an immediate best-seller. Meanwhile, Charles pursued an interest and skill in the field of medical research. As much as they tried to lead ordinary lives, however, the Lindberghs continued to gain unwanted attention from the press. By the end of 1935, Charles had had enough. In an effort to escape the constant attention, Charles, Anne, and their new young son, Jon, set sail for Europe. The Lindberghs were leaving America for a new home in another country.

I believe that with the assistance of people who must believe in my innocence – help that can be submitted by them by way of a defense fund which my attorneys must have if they are to success- fully carry out my appeal, my conviction can be overcome, and the records of this crime kept open so that the true kidnapper and murderer may yet be apprehended and dealt with as justice may require. I ask only justice and the help of the public only to the end that justice may be attained.

Bruno Richard Hauptmann

Written on February 15, 1935, this memo is an appeal to the public on behalf of Bruno Richard Hauptmann. Sent out after his conviction, the idea was to collect funds to pay for the continued work of Hauptmann's attorneys through the appeal process.

HAUPTMANN'S APPEAL

While the Lindberghs attempted to lead quiet, private lives in the days after the trial, Bruno Richard Hauptmann spent his time fighting for his life. Within moments after being sentenced to death, Hauptmann was led out of the courtroom; at that point his devoted wife, Anna, broke down in tears. Likewise, when Hauptmann reached his cell, he fell on his cot and sobbed. By the next day, however, he was back on his feet giving interviews and proclaiming his innocence.

Though there was a large amount of public sentiment against Hauptmann during and after the trial, there were also people who weren't convinced of his guilt. For instance, Eleanor Roosevelt, the wife of President Franklin Delano Roosevelt, publicly expressed her

Governor Harold G. Hoffman of New Jersey is shown signing a thirty-day reprieve for Bruno Richard Hauptmann in this photograph from January 16, 1936. Sentenced to die in the electric chair, Hauptmann was granted the reprieve for further investigation after the Supreme Court refused him a second appeal. Attorney General David Wilentz *(center)* and Assistant Prosecuting Attorney Anthony Hauck *(right)* stand at the side of Hoffman's desk in Trenton, New Jersey.

doubts about the outcome of the trial. Others staged rallies to help Hauptmann raise money to defend himself in appeal. At many of these events Anna Hauptmann was a featured speaker. With this support, the Hauptmanns fought for a new trial.

Hauptmann's case was reviewed. However, after two appeals were rejected, it looked like his case was going nowhere. At this point Hauptmann found an ally in New Jersey governor Harold G. Hoffman. Hoffman had been the only member of one appeals panel to vote to overturn the death sentence for Hauptmann. The governor believed that there was enough evidence to look into the matter further. Due to the governor's efforts, Hauptmann's execution was postponed a number of times. Eventually, though, the wheels of justice did grind onward. Hauptmann ran out of appeals and ran out of time. On April 3, 1936, Bruno Richard Hauptmann was strapped into the electric chair and put to death by the state of New Jersey.

Anna Hauptman receives word of her husband's execution in this photograph taken on April 3, 1936, in a Trenton, New Jersey, hotel room. Anna Hauptmann was loyal and steadfast and fought until the end to overturn her husband's conviction. When she heard that she had lost the battle at last, she collapsed tragically into the arms of *New York Daily Mirror* reporter Frank Doyle.

IMPACT ON HISTORY

Though the Lindbergh case ended with the execution of Bruno Richard Hauptmann, the debate over the trial did not die down. Until her death roughly sixty years after her husband's conviction, Anna Hauptmann struggled to clear his name. Moreover, in recent decades a number of people have investigated the case in an attempt to clarify whether Hauptmann was responsible for the kidnapping and death of Charles Lindbergh Jr. Some investigators have gone to great lengths to show how Hauptmann's trial was unfair, while others contend that Hauptmann could not have been the kidnapper. In fact, some have even gone so far as to say that the Lindberghs were somehow to blame and that the trial was a massive cover-up. The debate goes on.

One immediate result of the case was that Congress passed a new federal law, which was the first federal kidnapping law in America. Known as the Lindbergh Act or the Lindbergh Law, this law made it a federal offense to transport a kidnapping victim across state lines. Kidnapping also became a federal crime if the kidnappers used the

After the devastating trial for his son's murder, Charles Lindbergh moved his family overseas. They returned to the United States when World War II broke out. A committed pacifist, Lindbergh spoke out against his country's involvement in the war, which enraged President Franklin Delano Roosevelt. Later in his life, Lindbergh was active in the conservation movement. He is pictured here in the Philippines in 1970, a few years before his death.

postal service to send ransom notes. Another result of the Lindbergh case was the banning of cameras and microphones from courtrooms. Many argued that Hauptmann hadn't gotten a fair trial because of the distraction caused by the press.

After the trial, Lindbergh moved to Europe with his family. Unfortunately, he could not avoid the press or controversy altogether. In the years leading up to World War II, Lindbergh frequently visited

ANNE MORROW LINDBERGH

In the early days of their marriage, Anne and Charles Lindbergh flew around the world together. Charles taught Anne how to fly, and she became his copilot and navigator. Anne was also a talented writer. In time, she would publish many best-selling books, including *North to the Orient* and *Gift from the Sea*. Though she was married to one of the world's most famous men, Anne Morrow Lindbergh made a name for herself by becoming a highly successful author.

Germany, where he met with leaders of the Nazi Party and inspected German military aircraft. This caused a wave of negative publicity for Lindbergh. Then, after moving back to America in 1939, Lindbergh stirred up further controversy by urging America to stay out of the war, stating his belief that the German war machine was unbeatable. Even though Lindbergh had argued against America's involvement before the war, he did get involved in the war after the Japanese attack on Pearl Harbor. While serving as a technical advisor for the U.S. Air Force in the Pacific, Lindbergh flew on a number of combat missions.

Following World War II, Lindbergh continued to lead a life mostly out of the public eye. As he did throughout his life, Lindbergh spent much of his time serving as a consultant to the U.S. Air Force as well as to private air transportation companies. He also published *The Spirit of St. Louis,* the Pulitzer Prize–winning retelling of his historic flight from New York to Paris. In the later years of his life, Charles Lindbergh became heavily involved in the conservation movement. He died on August 26, 1974, at his home in Hawaii.

The Lindbergh kidnapping case grabbed the public's attention like nothing before it ever had. Because of Lindbergh's immense fame, the press converged on that small courthouse in Flemington and reported on every aspect of the trial. As the town and surrounding area became a tourist attraction, the trial became more and more of a spectacle. On the one side, there was Charles Lindbergh, sitting through nearly every minute of the trial and playing a crucial role in seeing that justice was done for the death of his son. On the other side, Bruno Richard Hauptmann was tried, convicted, and executed for a crime he claimed he didn't commit and for which many questions remain unanswered to this day. Though there have been many theories about what happened to the Lindbergh baby, there remains a tremendous amount of mystery surrounding the case. At this point it's unlikely that we'll ever know for sure what happened on that chilly night in March 1932.

GLOSSARY

alibi The claim of having been elsewhere when a crime was committed and thus being unable to have committed it.

arraignment To call an accused person before a court to answer the charge made against him or her.

aviation The operation of aircraft.

aviator A pilot.

defense The lawyer or team of lawyers representing a person accused of a crime, who is also known as the defendant.

deliberate To consider the facts presented in a trial before reaching a verdict.

indict To charge a person with committing a crime.

mistrial A trial that has no result, due to improper procedures or failure of the jury to reach a verdict.

prosecution The lawyer or team of lawyers attempting to prove that an accused person is guilty of a crime.

transatlantic Crossing the Atlantic Ocean.

unprecedented Never experienced before.

FOR MORE INFORMATION

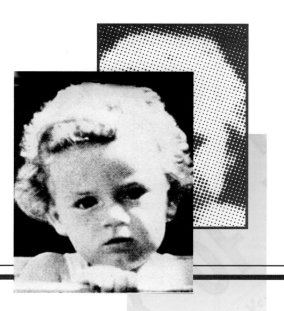

The Charles A. and Anne Morrow Lindbergh Foundation
2150 Third Avenue North, Suite 310
Anoka, MN 55303-2200
(763) 576-1596
Web site: http://www.lindberghfoundation.org

Smithsonian National Air and Space Museum
Smithsonian Institution
Seventh Street and Independence Avenue SW
Washington, DC 20560-0321
(202) 357-2700
Web site: http://www.nasm.si.edu

WEB SITES

Due to the changing nature of Internet links, the Rosen Publishing Group, Inc., has developed an online list of Web sites related to the subject of this book. This site is updated regularly. Please use this link to access the list:

http://www.rosenlinks.com/gttc/lbkt

FOR FURTHER READING

Berg, A. Scott. *Lindbergh*. New York: Berkley Publishing Group, 1998.

Edwards, Judith. *The Lindbergh Baby Kidnapping in American History.* Berkeley Heights, NJ: Enslow Publishers, 2000.

Fisher, Jim. *The Lindbergh Case.* New Brunswick, NJ: Rutgers University Press, 1987.

Lindbergh, Charles A. *The Spirit of St. Louis.* New York: Charles Scribner's Sons, 1953.

Monroe, Judy. *The Lindbergh Baby Kidnapping: A Headline Court Case.* Berkeley Heights, NJ: Enslow Publishers, 2000.

BIBLIOGRAPHY

Berg, A. Scott. *Lindbergh*. New York: Berkley Publishing Group, 1998.

Edwards, Judith. *The Lindbergh Baby Kidnapping in American History*. Berkeley Heights, NJ: Enslow Publishers, 2000.

Fisher, Jim. *The Ghosts of Hopewell: Setting the Record Straight in the Lindbergh Case*. Carbondale, IL: Southern Illinois University Press, 1999.

Fisher, Jim. *The Lindbergh Case*. New Brunswick, NJ: Rutgers University Press, 1987.

Kennedy, Ludovic. *The Airman and the Carpenter: The Lindbergh Kidnapping and the Framing of Richard Hauptmann*. New York: Viking Penguin, 1985.

Lindbergh, Charles A. *The Spirit of St. Louis*. New York: Charles Scribner's Sons, 1953.

Lindbergh, Reeve. *Under A Wing: A Memoir*. New York: Simon & Schuster, 1998.

Milton, Joyce. *Loss of Eden: A Biography of Charles and Anne Morrow Lindbergh*. New York: HarperCollins Publishers, 1993.

Monroe, Judy. *The Lindbergh Baby Kidnapping: A Headline Court Case*. Berkeley Heights, NJ: Enslow Publishers, 2000.

PRIMARY SOURCE IMAGE LIST

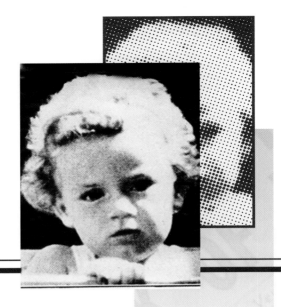

Cover: Photograph of Charles Lindbergh Jr. Taken in 1931.

Page 4: Poster for missing Charles Lindbergh Jr. From the U.S. Department of Justice. Created in March 1932.

Page 6: Photograph of Charles Lindbergh standing before the *Spirit of St. Louis*. Taken on May 21, 1927, in New York City.

Page 9: Photograph of Charles Lindbergh flying the *Spirit of St. Louis* over Paris. Taken on May 21, 1927, in Paris, France.

Page 10: Photograph of the *Spirit of St. Louis*, on display at the National Air and Space Museum. Taken in Washington, DC, in 2002.

Page 11: Photograph of a ticker-tape parade held in honor of Charles Lindbergh. Taken in New York City on June 13, 1927.

Page 12: Photograph of the Lindberghs. Taken on August 27, 1929, in Cleveland, Ohio.

Page 13: Photograph of Charles Lindbergh Jr. with his mother, grandmother, and great-grandmother. Taken in 1931.

Page 15: Still taken from a home movie of Betty Gow and Charles Lindbergh Jr. Taken on April 4, 1932.

Page 16: Photograph of reporters in front of the Lindbergh home. Taken on March 2, 1932, in Hopewell, New Jersey.

Page 17: Photograph of a police detective examining the Lindbergh home. Taken in March 1932, in Hopewell, New Jersey.

Page 18: Newspaper clipping reporting the kidnapping of Charles Lindbergh Jr. From March 1932.

Page 20: Display of kidnapping notes. Photographed September 24, 1934, in New York City. Photograph of John Condon. Taken December 27, 1934, in Flemington, New Jersey.

Page 23: Photograph of Robert Peacock, Anthony Hauck, and John Lamb with evidence. Taken on January 3, 1935, at the Hunterdon County Courthouse in Flemington, New Jersey.

Page 24: Photograph of H. W. Schwartzkopf. Taken on March 2, 1932, in Hopewell, New Jersey.

Page 25: Photograph of John Lyons and Walter Lyle. Taken on August 20, 1934, in New York City.

Page 26: Photograph of Bruno Hauptmann with police officials. Taken in New York City on September 19, 1934.

Page 29: Photograph of Judge Thomas W. Trenchard. Taken on January 21, 1935, in Flemington, New Jersey.

Pages 30–31: Diagram of Lindbergh kidnapping scene. Created on March 2, 1932.

Page 32: Photograph of Charles Lindbergh testifying in the Hunterdon County Courthouse. Taken on January 3, 1935, in Flemington, New Jersey.

Page 33: Photograph of Amandus Hochmuth. Taken in 1935 at the Hunterdon County Courthouse in Flemington, New Jersey.

Page 34: Photograph of James Clark Sellers testifying. Taken in January 1935 in the Hunterdon County Courthouse in Flemington, New Jersey.

Page 35: Handwriting specimens used in the Lindbergh trial. Created on January 12, 1935, in Flemington, New Jersey.

Page 36: Photograph of Joseph Bornmann carrying ladder into courtroom. Taken in Flemington, New Jersey.

Page 38: Photograph of Edward Reilly, Lloyd Fisher, Frederick Pope, Bruno Hauptmann, and Edgar Rosecrans. Taken on December 26, 1935, in Flemington, New Jersey.

Page 40: Photograph of Edward Reilly and Bruno Hauptmann. Taken on January 30, 1935, in Flemington, New Jersey.

Page 42: Photograph of Isidor Fisch. Taken in 1935.

Page 43: Photograph of wooden plank used as evidence in Lindbergh trial, 1935, in Flemington, New Jersey.

Page 47: Photograph of Bruno Hauptmann hearing guilty verdict. Taken on February 13, 1935, in Flemington, New Jersey.

Page 49: Appeal to the public for defense funds. Written by Bruno Hauptmann's attorneys on February 15, 1935, in Flemington, New Jersey.

Page 50: Photograph of Governor Harold Hoffman signing reprieve with David Wilentz and Anthony Hauck. Taken on January 16, 1936, in Trenton, New Jersey.

Page 51: Photograph of Frank Doyle and Anna Hauptmann. Taken April 3, 1936, in Trenton, New Jersey.

Page 53: Photograph of Charles Lindbergh. Taken in the Philippines in August 1970 by an Associated Press photographer.

Page 54: Photograph of Anne Morrow Lindbergh. Taken on July 11, 1929, in Wichita, Kansas.

INDEX

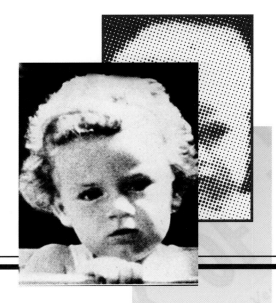

ABOUT THE AUTHOR

Greg Roensch is a writer who lives in San Francisco, California. His other books for young adults include *Football Hall of Famers: Vince Lombardi* and *Martial Arts Masters: Bruce Lee*.

CREDITS